THRONE
ROOM
CHALLENGE

PaRragon

Bath · New York · Cologne · Melbourne · Delhi
Hong Kong · Shenzhen · Singapore · Amsterdam

This edition published by Parragon Books Ltd in 2014

Parragon Books Ltd
Chartist House
15–17 Trim Street
Bath BA1 1HA, UK
www.parragon.com

Copyright © Parragon Books Ltd 2014
Individual puzzles © Any Puzzle Media Ltd

ISBN 978-1-4723-5918-6

Printed in China

Sit Down Quiz

1. On the Box

Name the sitcom character known for her joyfully sung ditty, 'Smelly Cat'.

2. Movie Magic

In what series of films does Tom Cruise play action hero, Ethan Hunt?

3. It's All Science

What was the name of the first human to journey into outer space? He made his historic journey in April 1961.

4. Sports Skills

In 2013, Andy Murray became the first British man to win the Wimbledon Men's Singles title for 77 years. But who was the last British woman to win the Wimbledon Ladies' Singles title, back in 1977?

Loose Vowels

All of the vowels have been flushed out of the following **capital cities**.

Can you work out what all of the words were originally?

LNDN

TTW

TKY

LM

MDRD

DDS BB

Rearranging

Join the word fragments together to make five complete words.

Each word in the finished list will be a **geographical feature**.

AND   ARC   ELA   GO

GRA   HIP   INS   LAC

LAG   MI   PEN   SSL

STA   STA   TE   TE

TI   ULA

Toilet Trivia

On Good Friday, 1930, the BBC replaced the news bulletin with an announcement that 'There is no news'. They then played some jolly piano music to fill the dead air.

M&M's chocolates are named after Forrest Mars, the son of the founder of the Mars chocolate company, and Bruce Murrie, the son of the founder of the Hershey chocolate company. That's why there's an apostrophe in the name.

Hamsters have a shorter pregnancy period than any other placental mammal – just 16 days! Each litter can contain 20 or more young, and the mother can become pregnant again immediately. Pet hamsters are all descended from a single brother and sister pairing made in the 1930s.

Pottering About

The letters in each of the following **UNESCO World Heritage Sites** have been mixed up.

Untangle each anagram to reveal the original words.

AEGRT ALLW FO ACHIN

AEGRT ABEIRRR EEFR

DENSYY AEOPR EHOSU

AESTTU FO BEILRTY

Film Buff

Can you work out the **film titles** represented by each set of initials? Each film is in IMDB.com's list of the top 250 highest-rated films of all time.

TSOTL

ROTLA

TLOTRTFOTR

SPR

BTTF

Cleaning Up

Decode the names of these **types of government** by shifting each letter a consistent amount forwards or backwards through the alphabet. For example, you might replace A with C, B with D, C with E and so on. The same code is used for every line.

MRLCJCXABQRY

JARBCXLAJLH

LXVVDWJURBV

VNARCXLAJLH

YUDCXLAJLH

Roll Call

Every other letter has been deleted from the following words. Can you use your skill and intuition to replace all of the missing letters?

Each item in the list is a **style of architecture**.

A_T_ _N_ _R_F_S

N_O_L_S_I_I_T

P_R_E_D_C_L_R

R_N_I_S_N_E

C_R_N_H_A_

B_Z_N_I_E

C_A_S_C_L

Sit Down Quiz

1. Musical Mulling

Which of the four Beatles was born first? And who was the youngest member of the group?

2. Movie Magic

Two films share the accolade of having the most Oscar nominations ever received for a single film. One was released in 1950, and the other in 1997. Can you name either?

3. It's All Science

Can you say which three precious metals are represented by the scientific element symbols Au, Ag and Pt – and which is which?

4. Sports Skills

Which team has won the FA Cup an impressive 11 times, more than any other team?

Loose Vowels

All of the vowels have been flushed out of the following **European languages**.

Can you work out what all of the words were originally?

CLNDC

NRWGN

KRNN

LBNN

STNN

TLN

Rearranging

Join the word fragments together to make five complete words.

Each word in the finished list will be a **part of the anatomy**.

AG   APP   ARY   AS

CAP   CRE   END   EST

ILL   INE   INT   IX

OES   OPH   PAN   US

Trivial Thoughts

Many interpretations have been given to the meaning of the '57 varieties' claim on Heinz bottles. The truth is that Henry Heinz, the company founder, chose 57 because it was his lucky number. It has no other meaning.

☆ ☆ ☆ ☆ ☆

Most of the planets rotate on their axis in an anticlockwise direction, the same as the sun. The two exceptions are Venus and Uranus, which rotate the other way.

☆ ☆ ☆ ☆ ☆

Walt Disney was scared of mice, despite creating possibly the most successful cartoon character ever, Mickey Mouse!

Pottering About

The letters in each of the following **science-fiction TV shows** have been mixed up.

Untangle each anagram to reveal the original words.

AABELRSTTT AAACCGILT

AEEHORSUW EEHINRTT

EHT GHIILTTW ENOZ

AMNQTUU AELP

Film Buff

Can you work out the **film titles** represented by each set of initials? Each film is in IMDB.com's list of the top 250 highest-rated films of all time.

JAN

TGE

AFOD

TNOTH

SLIH

Cleaning Up

Decode the names of **Santa's reindeer** by shifting each letter a consistent amount forwards or backwards through the alphabet. For example, you might replace A with C, B with D, C with E and so on. The same code is used for every line.

QAXIOTC

EGPCRTG

GJSDAEW

SPCRTG

SPHWTG

Roll Call

Every other letter has been deleted from the following words. Can you use your skill and intuition to replace all of the missing letters?

Each item in the list is **a famous volcano**.

S_N_O_I I

S_ _E_E_S

S_R_M_O_I

K_A_A_O_

V_S_V_U_

E_N_

F_J_

Sit Down Quiz

1. Around the World

Captain Cook first landed in Botany Bay, Australia, on the 29th of April in which year?

2. On the Box

Which two long-running sitcoms featured the same Boston- and then Seattle-based psychiatrist?

3. It's All Science

What is the name of the potentially deadly, odourless gas that is produced by incomplete combustion?

4. Sports Skills

Which team has won the FIFA World Cup more times than any other team, and in which year did they last win?

Loose Vowels

All of the vowels have been flushed out of the following **wedding anniversaries**.

Can you work out what all of the words were originally?

LTHR

CTTN

CHN

CRL

PPR

TN

Rearranging

Join the word fragments together to make five complete country names.

Each word in the finished list will be a **Latin American country**.

AD AGO AGU AND

ARG AY COL ELA

ENT EZU IA INA

NID OMB PAR TOB

TRI VEN

Trivial Thoughts

In 2005, the Queen exerted her rights to the ownership of 88 cygnets on the River Thames. They are now looked after by the official Swan Marker. The similar post of Royal Swan Keeper has existed since the 12th century.

The Lego group manufactures more rubber tyres each year than any other tyre manufacturer!

The record for the most Oscar nominators without a win is held by film composer Victor Young, who was nominated 21 times prior to winning. Ironically, he finally received an Oscar only after he had died!

Pottering About

The letters in each of the following **anatomical parts of a flower** have been mixed up.

Untangle each anagram to reveal the original words.

ACCEEELPRT

AAHLMSTU

ACELPR

AEMNST

AGIMST

AELPT

Film Buff

Can you work out the **film titles** represented by each set of initials? Each film is in IMDB.com's list of the top 250 highest-rated films of all time.

TDK

CHL

OUATIA

GWTW

TSS

Cleaning Up

Decode the English descriptions of these **signs of the Zodiac** by shifting each letter a consistent amount forwards or backwards through the alphabet. For example, you might replace A with C, B with D, C with E and so on. The same code is used for every line.

XLI EVGLIV

XLI WGEPIW

XLI FYPP

XLI GVEF

XLI JMWL

XLI PMSR

Roll Call

Every other letter has been deleted from the following words. Can you use your skill and intuition to replace all of the missing letters?

Each item in the list is a **woodwind instrument**.

C_R A_G A_S

D_D E_I O_

B_G I E_

C_A I E_

H_R P_P _

O_O_

Sit Down Quiz

1. On the Box

What is the name of the president portrayed in 'The West Wing' by Martin Sheen?

2. Movie Magic

Two actors have won two consecutive Oscar awards. Can you name either of them?

3. Around the World

Which is the longest river in the United Kingdom?

4. Sports Skills

Can you name the colours of the three rings in the top row of the Olympic Games logo?

Loose Vowels

All of the vowels have been flushed out of the following pieces of **body armour**.

Can you work out what all of the words and phrases were originally?

CHN ML

BCKPLT

NSPC

GNTLT

SRCT

HLMT

Rearranging

Rearrange and join the word fragments to make five **edible fish**.

AIT   ANG   DO   EL

ER   FI   FLO   HN

JO   KER   LER   MAC

RY   SH   TEB   UND

WHI

Trivial Thoughts

With Japanese households frequently short of physical space, some farmers now produce cube-shaped watermelons by growing them in glass boxes. This makes them easier to fit into fridges, and allows them to be stacked.

There is more fresh water in the atmosphere than in all of the rivers on the planet combined.

☆ ☆ ☆ ☆ ☆

William Henry Harrison, president of the US in 1841, died after just a month in office, having caught pneumonia during his inauguration speech by giving the longest such speech ever made. Delivered in the pouring rain, without a coat, it took him two hours to read the speech.

Pottering About

The letters in each of the following **Summer Olympic cities** have been mixed up.

Untangle each anagram to reveal the original city names.

AADEMMRST

AABCELNOR

BEELMNORU

CHKLMOOST

EHIIKLNS

AELMNORT

Film Buff

Can you work out the **film titles** represented by each set of initials? Each film is in IMDB.com's list of the top 250 highest-rated films of all time.

GWH

TKAM

TGTBATU

AAE

TUS

Cleaning Up

Decode the names of these **athletics events** by shifting each letter a consistent amount forwards or backwards through the alphabet. For example, you might replace A with C, B with D, C with E and so on. The same code is used for every line.

XKDTHUT CUJHUI

FEBU LQKBJ

IJUUFBUSXQIU

JHYFBU ZKCF

XUFJQJXBED

Roll Call

Every other letter has been deleted from the following words. Can you use your skill and intuition to replace all of the missing letters?

Each item in the list is a **type of shoe**.

M_C_A_I_

P_A_F_R_

P_I_S_L_

S_I_E_T_

S_I_P_R

S_E_K_R

34

Sit Down Quiz

1. Around the World

Mount Everest is the world's tallest mountain, at a height of 8,848 m (29,029 ft), but what is the world's second tallest mountain?

2. Movie Magic

What is the name of the fourth film released in the *Indiana Jones* movie series?

3. Musical Mulling

Which British pop duo had a number one hit in the UK pop chart in 1985 with 'West End Girls'?

4. Sports Skills

Can you name both of the players who have jointly won the most Men's Singles titles at Wimbledon in the Open Era (since 1968)?

Loose Vowels

All of the vowels have been flushed out of the following pieces of **laboratory equipment**.

Can you work out what all of the words were originally?

MCRSCP

DRPPR

PPTT

SPTL

BKR

TRPD

Rearranging

Join the word fragments together to make five complete words or phrases.

Each word or phrase in the finished list will be a **type of light bulb**.

AND   **CU**   **ENE**   **ENS**

ENT   **ESC**   **GH**   **GH**

HI   **HI**   **INC**   **ING**

INT   **ITY**   **IUM**   **MER**

OUR   **PRE**   **RE**   **RGY**

RY   **SAV**   **SOD**   **SSU**

VAP

Trivial Thoughts

Newborn babies have over 300 bones in their body, but these start to fuse together as they grow. By adulthood, there are only 206 separate bones in the human body.

Isaac Newton, the famous physicist and mathematician, spent much of his career focused on looking for hidden messages in the Bible. He also spent a considerable amount of time researching alchemy.

Flamingo's tongue was a special delicacy at the table of Roman emperors, where it was served in a dish that also included pheasant brains and parrotfish livers.

Pottering About

The letters in each of the following **board games** have been mixed up.

Untangle each anagram to reveal the original words.

ABEHILPSSTT

AABCGKMMNO

ADGHRSTU

LMNOOOPY

ABBCELRS

EEIRRSV

Film Buff

Can you work out the **film titles** represented by each set of initials? Each film is in IMDB.com's list of the top 250 highest-rated films of all time.

TWOO

TOE

AHX

TDH

FMJ

Cleaning Up

Decode the names of these **types of tea** by shifting each letter a consistent amount forwards or backwards through the alphabet. For example, you might replace A with C, B with D, C with E and so on. The same code is used for every line.

JSLQNXM GWJFPKFXY

QFUXFSL XTZHMTSL

WZXXNFS HFWFAFS

TWFSLJ UJPTJ

IFWOJJQNSL

Roll Call

Every other letter has been deleted from the following words. Can you use your skill and intuition to replace all of the missing letters?

Each item in the list is a type of **pasta**.

T_G_I_T_L_E

C_N_E_L_N_

S_A_H_T_I

F_R_A_L_

L_N_U_N_

R_G_T_N_

Sit Down Quiz

1. On the Box

In which five-season science fiction series did Bruce Boxleitner star as the commander of a distant space station?

2. Movie Magic

What is the name of Michael J Fox's character in the *Back to the Future* films?

3. Around the World

The River Amazon flows through seven countries. Which of them can you name?

4. Sports Skills

Mike Powell held the world record in which Summer Olympic discipline for a period of over 22 years?

Loose Vowels

All of the vowels have been flushed out of the following **types of tree**.

Can you work out what all of the words were originally?

CLYPTS
MGNL
PRCT
CCNT
SQ
CC

Rearranging

Rearrange and join the word fragments to make five **London attractions**.

ACE	AL	AM	ATO
BRI	BUC	CHA	DGE
ERV	GH	GUA	HOU
KIN	LEN	LIA	ME
MIL	NG	NGI	NI
NT	OBS	OF	OF
PAL	PAR	RD	ROY
RY	SES	THE	UM

Trivial Thoughts

If you've ever stared at a sudoku puzzle and wondered just how few numbers are required to get started, the answer is 17. With less than that many given numbers, the puzzle wouldn't have a unique solution.

Honeybees dance to show the location of flowers, waggling their behinds in various figures of eight in order to indicate the precise location of interesting nectar and pollen, water sources or even new hive locations.

It's frequently claimed that a human sneeze can leave the body at over 160 km/h (100 mph). The reality is much slower, although still impressive, being closer to 65 km/h (40 mph).

Pottering About

The letters in each of the following **vegetables** have been mixed up.

Untangle each anagram to reveal the original words.

ACEFILLORUW

AAAGPRSSU

CEENORSTW

BCCEMRUU

HMMOORSU

AABBCEG

Film Buff

Can you work out the **film titles** represented by each set of initials? Each film is in IMDB.com's list of the top 250 highest-rated films of all time.

TPB

OUATITW

TPOBAW

LDV

ITW

Cleaning Up

Decode the names of these **US state capitals** by shifting each letter a consistent amount forwards or backwards through the alphabet. For example, you might replace A with C, B with D, C with E and so on. The same code is used for every line.

WDOODKDVVHH

VDFUDPHQWR

QDVKYLOOH

KRQROXOX

ERVWRQ

Roll Call

Every other letter has been deleted from the following names. Can you use your skill and intuition to replace all of the missing letters?

Each item in the list is the name of a **legendary hero**.

D_V_ _R_C_E_T

R_B_N H_O_

A_A_E_N_N

G_L_A_E_H

A_H_L_E_

B_U_I_C_

L_N_E_O_

Sit Down Quiz

1. On the Box

Which actress played teenage witch Willow Rosenberg in 'Buffy the Vampire Slayer'?

2. Movie Magic

Which man won more Oscars than any other person? His personal total amounted to 26 Oscars – 22 competitive and 4 honorary.

3. Around the World

How many of the six countries which border on to the Black Sea can you name?

4. Sports Skills

Which champion athlete has won more Olympic gold medals than any other person?

Loose Vowels

All of the vowels have been flushed out of the following **types of vehicle**.

Can you work out what all of the words were originally?

CRVNTT

GLF CRT

TRCTR

SLDG

TNDM

Rearranging

Rearrange and join the word fragments to make the names of five **countries**.

AKH **AN** **BAN** **BUR**

DE **EMB** **FA** **GLA**

KAZ **KI** **LUX** **NA**

ND **OU** **RG** **RLA**

SH **SO** **ST** **SWI**

TZE

Trivial Thoughts

According to medical reports, one in 18 men has a third nipple, while only one in 50 women do. These typically look much more like a mole than a regular nipple, however.

☆☆☆☆☆

Some types of oak tree do not start producing acorns until they are 20 years old, and some do not do so until they have been growing for 50 years!

It's illegal to go out in public in Thailand unless you're wearing underwear.

Pottering About

The letters in each of the following **cheeses** have been mixed up.

Untangle each anagram to reveal the original names.

AEFGMOR AFIRS

DER CEEEILRST

ADEEELLNSWY

ACEHILLPRY

AGGLNOOORZ

AACEHILNRS

Film Buff

Can you work out the **film titles** represented by each set of initials? Each film is in IMDB.com's list of the top 250 highest-rated films of all time.

LSATSB

BATB

VFV

TPS

TLOO

Cleaning Up

Decode the names of these **colours** by shifting each letter a consistent amount forwards or backwards through the alphabet. For example, you might replace A with C, B with D, C with E and so on. The same code is used for every line.

OPMLPJDNZ

HVBZIOV

DIYDBJ

JMVIBZ

QDJGZO

TZGGJR

Roll Call

Every other letter has been deleted from the following words. Can you use your skill and intuition to replace all of the missing letters?

Each item in the list is a **cut of beef**.

F_A_ _R_N S_E_K

S_O_L_E_ _E_D_R

F_L_T M_G_O_

T_P S_R_O_N

S_A_E R_B_

S_L_E_S_D_

Sit Down Quiz

1. On the Box

Which actor played oil tycoon J R Ewing in the original series of 'Dallas'?

2. Movie Magic

Which 1982 sword-and-sorcery film provided a breakthrough role for Arnold Schwarzenegger?

3. It's All Science

Three metallic elements have chemical symbols which derive from the word for 'silver' in various languages. Can you name them?

4. Sports Skills

In which year, and in what city, were the first modern Olympics held?

Loose Vowels

All of the vowels have been flushed out of the following **flavours**.

Can you work out what all of the words were originally?

CHCLT
LQRC
NSD
CRML
RNG
PPL

Rearranging

Join the word fragments together to make the names of five **English counties**.

AT BUC CHE ER

ER GHA GLO GRE

HI IRE IRE IRE

KIN KSH MAN MPT

MSH NOR NOR ONS

RE RSH ST STE

TH THA UCE YOR

Trivial Thoughts

You might know how many megabytes or gigabytes your phone or other device has – and that's millions or billions of bytes. But did you know that half a byte is called a 'nybble'? And that a quarter of a 'nybble' is a 'bit'?

☆ ☆ ☆ ☆ ☆

The British statute book once forbade eating mince pies on Christmas Day, between around 1640 and 1660. At the time, Oliver Cromwell's puritanical parliament had enacted a range of legislation that banned people from celebrating Christmas.

☆ ☆ ☆ ☆ ☆

In Australia, it is illegal not to vote in a federal election or referendum. If voters cannot give an acceptable reason for failing to vote, they can be sent to court. The court can then issue a fine and record a criminal conviction against them.

Pottering About

Untangle the following anagrams to reveal five **subjects you might study at school.**

EHMO CCEIMNOOS
ACILOS CCEEINS
CHIPSSY
ACCLLSUU
EEGMORTY
EGHILNS

Film Buff

Can you work out the **film titles** represented by each set of initials? Each film is in IMDB.com's list of the top 250 highest-rated films of all time.

TDKR

OFOTCN

HTTYD

WAOVW

TEM

Cleaning Up

Decode the names of these **British Prime Ministers** by shifting each letter a consistent amount forwards or backwards through the alphabet. For example, you might replace A with C, B with D, C with E and so on. The same code is used for every line.

DDGQV YWGJYW

UZSETWJDSAF

USDDSYZSF

UZMJUZADD

YDSVKLGFW

LZSLUZWJ

Roll Call

Every other letter has been deleted from the following words. Can you use your skill and intuition to replace all of the missing letters?

Each item in the list is **a type of law of governance**.

I_T_R_A_I_N_L

F_N_N_I_L

C_N_R_C_

C_I_I_A_

M_L_T_R_

P_O_E_T_

66

Sit Down Quiz

1. On the Box

Name the US sitcom which follows the dysfunctional lives of the members of the Bluth family.

2. Movie Magic

Which 1995 political romcom starred Michael Douglas and Annette Bening as the lead couple?

3. Musical Mulling

Which pop song holds the record for the most consecutive weeks spent at the top of the UK singles chart? Who was the artist?

4. Sports Skills

Can you name both of the two teams who have won consecutive FIFA World Cups?

Loose Vowels

All of the vowels have been flushed out of the following **percussion instruments**.

Can you work out what all of the words were originally?

CLST

MRMB

TMPN

TM-TM

BNGS

CHMS

Rearranging

Join the word fragments together to reveal five **breeds of dog**.

AN AT CHI CK
COC DA EL ERA
GRE HUA HUA JA
KER LL NE NI
NI POM RUS SE
SPA

Trivial Thoughts

Search behemoth Google is so-called thanks to the poor spelling of one of its founders. They intended it to be called Googol, after the very large number – one followed by a hundred zeroes – but accidentally registered the wrong domain and so decided to stick with the name.

'Typewriter' is often claimed to be the longest word that can be spelt using a single row of a regular QWERTY keyboard. While there seems to be no longer word, 'typewriter' is not unique – we also found 'perpetuity', 'prerequire', 'proprietor' and 'repertoire'.

If you're now wondering what the longest words you can spell with other lines of the keyboard are, the answer is that the longest word that can be made using only the middle row is 'alfalfas'. The bottom row can't make any words at all, no matter how short!

Pottering About

The letters in each of the following **fruits** have been mixed up.

Untangle each anagram to reveal the original words.

CEEEILMNNT

ABERRRSTWY

AEELMNORTW

ACEEINNRT

AEEILNPPP

AEGNOR

Film Buff

Can you work out the **film titles** represented by each set of initials? Each film is in IMDB.com's list of the top 250 highest-rated films of all time.

DSHILTSWALTB

TBL

TBOTRK

IHON

TBU

Cleaning Up

Decode the names of these **Renaissance artists** by shifting each letter a consistent amount forwards or backwards through the alphabet. For example, you might replace A with C, B with D, C with E and so on. The same code is used for every line.

EAUZWDSFYWDG

TGLLAUWDDA

VS NAFUA

ZGDTWAF

JSHZSWD

Roll Call

Every other letter has been deleted from the following words. Can you use your skill and intuition to replace all of the missing letters?

Each item in the list is a type of **religion**.

P_O_E_T_N_I_M

C_N_U_I__N_S_

C_T_O_I_I_M

C_L_I_I_M

M_T_O_I_M

M_R_O_I_M

B_D_H_S_

Sit Down Quiz

1. On the Box

Which musical comedy-drama television series is primarily set at William McKinley High School?

2. Movie Magic

The title of Oscar-winning film *Eternal Sunshine of the Spotless Mind* is taken from a poem by which 18th-century English poet?

3. Around the World

Which is the world's most populous city, measured according to official city boundaries?

4. Sports Skills

The USA has held the most modern Olympic games, hosting eight events in total. Which country is in second place, having hosted the games on five occasions?

Loose Vowels

All of the vowels have been flushed out of the following **elemental gases**.

Can you work out what all of the words were originally?

CHLRN

FLRN

HLM

RGN

RDN

NN

Rearranging

Join the word fragments together to make five complete words or phrases.

Each word or phrase in the finished list will be a **type of book**.

AP   AUT   BIO   DIA

DIC   EL   ENC   GRA

GRA   HY   IC   NA

NOV   OBI   OGR   OPE

PH   PHY   RY   TIO

YCL

Trivial Thoughts

Only 3% of the water on Earth is fresh. The remaining 97% is salt water.

Flamingos can only feed when their head is upside down, which is why their jaws and tongue are reversed compared to other birds.

When Egypt was first being colonized, there was such a glut of mummies that they were used for all kinds of unusual purposes. Pharmaceutical products were a particularly popular use, and mummies were also used to form the brown pigment 'mummy brown', also known as 'Egyptian brown'.

Pottering About

The letters in each of the following **team sports** have been mixed up.

Untangle each anagram to reveal the original words.

AABBEKLLST

AERTW LOOP

BBEGHILOS

ACELORSS

DENORRSU

CGILNRU

CEHKOY

Film Buff

Can you work out the **film titles** represented by each set of initials? Each film is in IMDB.com's list of the top 250 highest-rated films of all time.

MPATHG
TSR
TMWSLV
TWBB
IAWL

Cleaning Up

Decode the names of these **London Underground lines** by shifting each letter a consistent amount forwards or backwards through the alphabet. For example, you might replace A with C, B with D, C with E and so on. The same code is used for every line.

OGVTQRQNKVCP

RKEECFKNNA

DCMGTNQQ

FKUVTKEV

PQTVJGTP

Roll Call

Every other letter has been deleted from the following words. Can you use your skill and intuition to replace all of the missing letters?

Each item in the list is **the name of a sea**.

E_S_ _H_N_

C_R_B_E_N

A_R_A_I_

A_A_I_N

C_S_I_N

A_G_A_

Sit Down Quiz

1. On the Box

Which BBC television series is the world's longest-running current affairs documentary programme?

2. Movie Magic

Which 2003 movie won all 11 Oscar categories it was nominated in, setting a record for the highest 'clean sweep' of all nominations?

3. Musical Mulling

Which Australian pop songstress had a number one UK hit in 1989 with 'Hand On Your Heart'?

4. Sports Skills

As of 2014, the USA has won 2,400 medals at the Summer Olympics. Ignoring countries that no longer exist, which country is in second place in the overall Summer medal rankings?

Loose Vowels

All of the vowels have been flushed out of the following **US states**.

Can you work out what all of the names were originally?

RKNSS
CLRD
LLNS
KLHM
LBM
RZN

Rearranging

Join the word fragments together to make five complete words or phrases.

Each word or phrase in the finished list will be the name of a **job**.

ACC   AN   BEA   CI

EFI   ER   ERI   FIR

GHT   IAL   IAN   KER

NAR   NT   OUN   SOC

TA   UTI   VET   WOR

Trivial Thoughts

Over 650 million bottles of Heinz Ketchup are sold each year, in over 140 different countries. That's a lot of tomato sauce!

☆ ☆ ☆ ☆ ☆

Thanks to a Royal Prerogative from 1324, any whale or sturgeon found on the British coast belongs to the monarch. Even if the monarch gives permission to keep it, it is still illegal to sell it.

☆ ☆ ☆ ☆ ☆

Trinity Church in New York City, at the junction of Wall Street and Broadway, has a royal charter dating from 1697 that gives it control over any whales washing up on the banks of the city. The church still maintains this claim.

Pottering About

The letters in each of the following **vehicles** have been mixed up.

Untangle each anagram to reveal the original words.

EIPPRT CKRTU

AEELLMORRST

AAEELNOPR

AABCELMNU

BEIKMOORT

BIIMNSU

Film Buff

Can you work out the **film titles** represented by each set of initials? Each film is in IMDB.com's list of the top 250 highest-rated films of all time.

ITNOTF

TBS

SITR

LOUATII

TTS

Cleaning Up

Decode the names of these **Elvis Presley songs** by shifting each letter a consistent amount forwards or backwards through the alphabet. For example, you might replace A with C, B with D, C with E and so on. The same code is used for every line.

VGRVTN JI HT HDIY

CZVMOWMZVF CJOZG

GJIZNJHZ OJIDBCO

NPNKDXDJPN HDIYN

OCVO'N VGG MDBCO

Roll Call

Every other letter has been deleted from the following words. Can you use your skill and intuition to replace all of the missing letters?

Each item in the list is a **fairy tale character**.

L_T_L_ _I_S M_F_E_

F_I_Y G_D_O_H_R

P_I_C_ _H_R_I_G

R_M_E_S_I_T_K_N

S_E_P_N_ _E_U_Y

B_G B_D W_L_

Sit Down Quiz

1. On the Box

Who is the well-known British comedy writer that connects sitcom 'Coupling' to sci-fi adventure series 'Doctor Who'?

2. Movie Magic

How many film sequels have been made to *Jaws*, the 1975 film featuring a terrifying great white shark?

3. Musical Mulling

'Mambo No. 5' first reached number one in the UK singles chart with Lou Bega in 1999. Which act saw it climb to number one a second time, in 2001?

4. Sports Skills

Can you name the winner of the most consecutive Ladies' Singles titles at Wimbledon in the Open Era (since 1968)?

Loose Vowels

All of the vowels have been flushed out of the following **animals**.

Can you work out what all of the words were originally?

GN PG

RMDLL

NTTR

GN

LLM

MS

Rearranging

Join the word fragments together to reveal the names of five **national airlines**.

AIR AIR AIR AIR

AIR AN AR BRI

ES ES GAP JAP

LA LIN LIN ND

NEW ORE QAT SH

SIN TI WA WA

YS YS ZEA

Trivial Thoughts

The phrase 'raining cats and dogs' is of uncertain provenance, but its most likely explanation is a reference to the lack of sanitary disposal in early industrial Britain, when dead animals would literally wash down the road during heavy rain.

If you were to wear glasses which turned the entire world upside down, it's a remarkable fact that your brain would adapt to this new viewpoint within as little as five days. Everything would then appear right-side-up! But don't try this at home – it caused one psychologist to go mad when they later removed them!

If you died in the Houses of Parliament, you would come under the jurisdiction of the royal household's coroner since officially it remains a royal palace. It is often claimed this also entitles you to a state funeral, but unsurprisingly this is not true.

Pottering About

The letters in each of the following **amphibians** have been mixed up.

Untangle each anagram to reveal the original words.

INOOPS ADRT FGOR

BGINORRUW ADOT

AAADELMNRS

ALLOOTX

Film Buff

Can you work out the **film titles** represented by each set of initials? Each film is in IMDB.com's list of the top 250 highest-rated films of all time.

TWOWS

ITMFL

MOM

SOAT

MNT

Cleaning Up

Decode the names of these **British Kings** by shifting each letter a consistent amount forwards or backwards through the alphabet. For example, you might replace A with C, B with D, C with E and so on. The same code is used for every line.

JOHYSLZ

DPSSPHT

HSMYLK

LKDHYK

OLUYF

Roll Call

Every other letter has been deleted from the following words. Can you use your skill and intuition to replace all of the missing letters?

Each item in the list is **a type of knot**.

H_L_ _I_C_

S_E_P_H_N_

C_O_H_T

W_N_S_R

D_U_L_

G_A_N_

Sit Down Quiz

1. Around the World

Estonia shares a land border with Russia and which other country?

2. Movie Magic

Which political thriller won both Best Film at the BAFTAs and Best Picture at the Oscars in 2013?

3. It's All Science

The nucleus of a hydrogen atom consists of which subatomic particle?

4. Sports Skills

Which country holds the record for the longest gap between winning FIFA World Cups?

Loose Vowels

All of the vowels have been flushed out of the following **items of clothing**.

Can you work out what all of the words were originally?

WSTCT

SWTR

BLS

FLC

KMN

CLK

Rearranging

Rearrange and join the word fragments to make five types of **gym equipment**.

AL   AN   BA   CE

CRO   ELL   ER   ER

ER   HI   IC   IN

IN   ING   IPT   IST

MAC   ND   NE   PRE

RES   ROW   SHO   SS

SS   TRA   TRA   ULD

Trivial Thoughts

The classic time-travel film *Back to the Future* nearly had a much stranger name. A studio executive was determined to rename it to *Spaceman from Pluto*, arguing that no successful film could have 'future' in its title.

In 1904, Hippolyte Aucouturier found a novel method to help him cycle the Tour de France – he used a car to tow him along the road! Unfortunately, this proved a little too obvious, and he was disqualified.

'Play it again, Sam' is a famous quotation from the 1942 film, *Casablanca*. Unfortunately, the line is never actually spoken in the film, although both 'Play it once, Sam' and 'Play it, Sam' are both said by Ingrid Bergman's character, Ilsa Lund, who also says 'Sing it, Sam'.

Pottering About

The letters in each of the following **pop groups** have been mixed up.

Untangle each anagram to reveal the original names.

CEHIMRSTUY

ACDLLOPY

EEFILSTW

EEGINSS

AIOSS

EENQU

Film Buff

Can you work out the **film titles** represented by each set of initials? Each film is in IMDB.com's list of the top 250 highest-rated films of all time.

RFAD

MDB

TLOTRTROTK

WFTP

DMFM

Decode the names of these **famous French men and women** by shifting each letter a consistent amount forwards or backwards through the alphabet. For example, you might replace A with C, B with D, C with E and so on. The same code is used for every line.

WJYXUNXW KXWJYJACN

LQJAUNB MN PJDUUN

JUNGJWMAN MDVJB

KARPRCCN KJAMXC

PDBCJEN NROONU

Roll Call

Every other letter has been deleted from the following words. Can you use your skill and intuition to replace all of the missing letters?

Each item in the list is **a word that can be used to describe a plant**.

E_E_G_E_N

P_R_N_I_L

C_I_B_R

S_P_I_G

C_R_A_

F_O_E_

Sit Down Quiz

1. Musical Mullings

Which long-running musical theatre show is based on a novel by French writer Gaston Leroux?

2. Movie Magic

Which child actress, later known for a range of romantic comedies, was first propelled to international fame by her starring role in *E.T. the Extra-Terrestrial*?

3. It's All Science

In chemistry, what range of pH levels do the acids cover?

4. Sports Skills

In cricket, what is the Ashes trophy reputed to contain?

Loose Vowels

All of the vowels have been flushed out of the following things that you might find in a **garden pond**.

Can you work out what all of the words were originally?

FNTN

TDPL

TD

STNS

LLY

Rearranging

Rearrange and join the word fragments together to reveal five **Bond villains**.

AL   AL   AL   CAR

DOM   EC   ELL   ENE

ER   ER   GEN   GEN

GRE   IC   IN   IOT

MED   NO   ORL   OV

RA   TRE   VEL   VER

YAN

Trivial Thoughts

Isaac Newton originally divided the rainbow into five colours: red, yellow, green, blue and violet. Only later did he split it into seven, out of the belief that seven was a universal magic number: seven days, seven planets, as then known, and seven musical notes (A–G).

Generations of children who have wondered why indigo and violet count as separate colours may be relieved to know that Newton himself made this observation:
'It is customary to list indigo as a colour lying between blue and violet, but it has never seemed to me that indigo is worth the dignity of being considered a separate colour. To my eyes it seems merely deep blue'.

John Wayne is the most successful leading man of all time, having had more lead roles in films than any other actor. He has had top billing a staggering 142 times!

Pottering About

The letters in each of the following **puzzles** have been mixed up.

Untangle each anagram to reveal the original words.

OPST EHT CDEEEFFINR
ACDEHORRSW
CDOORRSSW
FHIIKOSTU
DKOSUU
AEMZ

Film Buff

Can you work out the **film titles** represented by each set of initials? Each film is in IMDB.com's list of the top 250 highest-rated films of all time.

LOB

ACO

BCATSK

TGOW

TMF

Cleaning Up

Decode the names of these **famous operas** by shifting each letter a consistent amount forwards or backwards through the alphabet. For example, you might replace A with C, B with D, C with E and so on. The same code is used for every line.

GJHZWMK AF LZW MFVWJOGJDV

LZW TSJTWJ GX KWNADDW

ESVSEW TMLLWJXDQ

VAVG SFV SWFWSK

UGKA XSF LMLLW

Roll Call

Every other letter has been deleted from the following words. Can you use your skill and intuition to replace all of the missing letters?

Each item in the list is a **famous ballet**.

T_E S_E_P_N_ _E_U_Y

T_L_S O_ _O_F_A_

T_E N_T_R_C_E_

L_S S_L_H_D_S

C_N_E_E_L_

S_A_ _A_E

C_R_E_

Sit Down Quiz

1. On the Box

The first episode of long-running BBC soap 'EastEnders' was broadcast on 19th February of which year?

2. Around the World

Where on the Earth is the lowest point on dry land?

3. It's All Science

Which Italian physicist gave his name to the SI unit of electrical potential difference?

4. Sports Skills

Which athlete was the first to run a mile (1.6 km) in less than four minutes?

Loose Vowels

All of the vowels have been flushed out of the following **parts of a car**.

Can you work out what all of the words were originally?

CCLRTR

DMTR

RDTR

SNRF

NGN

DR

Rearrange and join the word fragments to reveal five **photographic accessories.**

ABO   AR   ARI   ARI

BAT   CHA   CIR   CUL

EA   ER   ER   FIL

LEC   LIC   NG   PAR

POL   POL   REF   REL

RG   RY   SE   SHU

TE   TER   TOR   TT

ZER   ZI

Trivial Thoughts

George Lucas was certain that the original *Star Wars* film would be a failure, so he went on holiday instead of attending the film's premiere!

The LEGO™ name is based on the first two letters of the Danish words, *Leg godt*, meaning 'play well'. It's just coincidence that in Latin it can be translated as 'I put together'!

There are only three official carpeted Great Seals of the United States of America in the world. One is in the Oval Office of the White House, and another is at the Liberty Bell in Philadelphia. The third is part of a Disney World attraction! An Act of the US Congress was required to allow it.

Pottering About

The letters in each of the following **burger toppings** have been mixed up.

Untangle each anagram to reveal the original words.

AAEIMNNOSY

AACDOOV

EGHIKNR

CEHKPTU

CEELTTU

ADMRSTU

Film Buff

Can you work out the **film titles** represented by each set of initials? Each film is in IMDB.com's list of the top 250 highest-rated films of all time.

TKS

LSOE

OTW

TSITE

GOTF

Cleaning Up

Decode the names of these **UK football clubs** by shifting each letter a consistent amount forwards or backwards through the alphabet. For example, you might replace A with C, B with D, C with E and so on. The same code is used for every line.

XBLLUZ WHYR YHUNLYZ

THUJOLZALY BUPALK

AVALUOHT OVAZWBY

ISHJRIBYU YVCLYZ

IVSAVU DHUKLYZ

Roll Call

Every other letter has been deleted from the following words. Can you use your skill and intuition to replace all of the missing letters?

Each item in the list is a **branch of medicine**.

P_A_T_C S_R_E_Y

A_A_S_H_T_C_

N_U_O_U_G_R_

D_R_A_O_O_Y_

I_M_N_L_G_

P_Y_H_A_R_

C_I_O_O_Y

Sit Down Quiz

1. On the Box

Which 2001 miniseries, set during World War Two, dramatized the history of a US parachute regiment, and was based on a factual book by Stephen E Ambrose?

2. Movie Magic

Which Oscar-winning British actor, born in 1960, is perhaps best known for roles in *Pride and Prejudice*, *Bridget Jones's Diary* and *The King's Speech*?

3. It's All Science

Which gas, sometimes also referred to as 'marsh gas', is the major component of natural gas, comprising about 87% of it by volume?

4. Sports Skills

Which Jamaican athlete broke his own 100-m sprint speed record both in August 2008 and then again in August 2009?

Loose Vowels

All of the vowels have been flushed out of the following **African countries**.

Can you work out what all of the countries were originally?

MDGSCR

MRTS

THP

LGR

RTR

MRCC

Rearranging

Rearrange and join the word fragments together to reveal the names of five **constellations**.

ARI   CAN   CAN   CAP

CAS   IA   IS   IS

ITT   MAJ   MIN   OR

OR   ORN   PE   RIC

SAG   SIO   US   US

Trivial Thoughts

The record for the largest Rugby World Cup win is a whopping 142–0! This feat was achieved by Australia in 2003, when they defeated Namibia.

Monopoly is probably the most successful commercial board game of all time. More than 275 million sets have been sold worldwide and it is available in 111 countries. It's also been translated into 43 different languages.

Monopoly inspires such devotion that the longest-recorded game lasted an amazing 70 consecutive days, while the most expensive version of the game ever made featured a 23-carat-gold game board and diamond-encrusted dice!

Pottering About

The letters in each of the following **Biblical apostles** have been mixed up.

Untangle each anagram to reveal the original names.

ABEHLMOORTW

AAHIMSTT

ADENRW

AHMOST

AEJMS

ADJSU

Film Buff

Can you work out the **film titles** represented by each set of initials? Each film is in IMDB.com's list of the top 250 highest-rated films of all time.

ESOTSM

ABM

BCWC

NCFOM

FAA

Cleaning Up

Decode the names of these **dairy products** by shifting each letter a consistent amount forwards or backwards through the alphabet. For example, you might replace A with C, B with D, C with E and so on. The same code is used for every line.

FRZV-FXVZZRQ ZVYX

PERZR SENVPUR

SEBZNTR SENVF

JUVCCRQ PERNZ

OHGGRE

Roll Call

Every other letter has been deleted from the following words. Can you use your skill and intuition to replace all of the missing letters?

Each item in the list is an **alcoholic spirit**.

M_L_ _H_S_Y

T_I_L_ _E_

F_A_B_I_E

W_I_E R_M

A_A_E_T_

S_H_A_P_

Sit Down Quiz

1. On the Box

What is the subtitle of Wallace and Gromit's first adventure, first broadcast on Christmas Eve, 1990?

2. Around the World

Which city is the capital of Tasmania, the island state located off the south coast of Australia?

3. It's All Science

What is the name of the sub-area of algebra concerned with the study of variables whose values can be only 'true' or 'false'?

4. Musical Mulling

Which former Girls Aloud member later became a judge on the 'The X Factor'?

Loose Vowels

All of the vowels have been flushed out of the following **migrating animals**.

Can you work out what all of the words were originally?

CND GS

WHPR SWN

SHRWTR

WLDBST

CRB

SLMN

Rearranging

Join the word fragments together to make five complete words.

Each word in the finished list will be a **type of bag**.

ASE ATH BAC BRI

CK CK EFC GER

IC KPA KSA LET

MES RUC SEN

Trivial Thoughts

In the two years after puberty, the human brain loses an average of 5,000 brain cell connections *per second*! This massive spring clean tidies up the brain at the point when it thinks we have learnt all of the most important things, such as how to use language.

A small number of words have multiple meanings, such that they can also be their own opposites! Examples include:
'dust' – to add dust, or to remove dust
'overlook' – to pay attention to, or to ignore.

There are 6,670,903,752,021,072,936,960 (6.67×10^{21}) possible different solutions to a sudoku. Each of these also has an extremely large number of possible puzzles that result in that solution. It's therefore extraordinarily unlikely that you will encounter the same puzzle twice, just by chance!

Pottering About

The letters in each of the following **types of building** have been mixed up.

Untangle each anagram to reveal the original words.

ABEOORRSTVY
EGHHILOSTU
ACEKPRRSSY
ABEHOOSTU
AACDEHLRT
AEMNORSTY

Film Buff

Can you work out the **film titles** represented by each set of initials? Each film is in IMDB.com's list of the top 250 highest-rated films of all time.

SWEVTESB

MAM

DDA

TDBATB

HMC

Cleaning Up

Decode the names of these **nationalities** by shifting each letter a consistent amount forwards or backwards through the alphabet. For example, you might replace A with C, B with D, C with E and so on. The same code is used for every line.

QKIJHQBYQD

ZQFQDUIU

RHYJYIX

SXYDUIU

YJQBYQD

Roll Call

Every other letter has been deleted from the following words. Can you use your skill and intuition to replace all of the missing letters?

Each item in the list is a **musical instrument**.

S_A_E_ _H_S_L_

F_E_C_ _O_N

H_R_S_C_O_D

K_T_L_D_U_

A_C_R_I_N

B_G_I_E

C_A_I_E_

Sit Down Quiz

1. On the Box

What was the name of the assistant detective in 'Inspector Morse' who later went on to have his own self-titled series?

2. Movie Magic

Which was the first animated film to be nominated for Best Picture at the Oscars?

3. Around the World

What name is given to the monumental statues found on Easter Island in the Pacific Ocean?

4. Sports Skills

Which English football team's home stadium is named the 'Stadium of Light'?

Loose Vowels

All of the vowels have been flushed out of the following **make-up products**.

Can you work out what all of the words were originally?

GRSPNT

FNDTN

YLNR

LPSTCK

MSCR

RG

Rearranging

Rearrange and join the word fragments to make five **elementary particles**.

AN	ANT	ANT	ANT
ANT	ARK	ARK	ARK
BOT	CHA	CTR	ELE
GE	INE	INO	IQU
IQU	IQU	MU	NEU
NO	ON	ON	RM
STR	TOM	TRI	UTR

Trivial Thoughts

The fruit-based mincemeat filling used in mince pies has no meat in it, but this has not always been the case. Until as recently as 100 years ago, a range of minced meats were frequently included in mince pies.

The first crossword was published in 1913 in the *New York World*. It was called 'Word-Cross' and had a simple diamond-shaped grid. It later caught on in Britain, but *The Times* of London held out from publishing one until 1930. For a while it also published a Latin version, describing the English puzzle as failing to meet its 'exacting intellectual standard'.

William Howard Taft has the unique distinction of being the heaviest US President ever. He weighed over 135 kg (300 lb), and once got stuck in the White House bath. The bath was replaced with a larger one, to avoid a potential repeat embarrassment!

Pottering About

The letters in each of the following **currencies** have been mixed up.

Untangle each anagram to reveal the original words.

AACDHMR

ADLLOR

CDEOSU

ADINR

ACFNR

EKNOR

Film Buff

Can you work out the **film titles** represented by each set of initials? Each film is in IMDB.com's list of the top 50 **highest-rated romantic comedies** of all time.

SLP

SIL

HJNTIY

FSM

TSN

Cleaning Up

Decode the names of these **gases** by shifting each letter a consistent amount forwards or backwards through the alphabet. For example, you might replace A with C, B with D, C with E and so on. The same code is used for every line.

ZQVJGYWF UZDGJAVW

USJTGF VAGPAVW

FALJGMK GPAVW

SEEGFAS

ZWDAME

145

Roll Call

Every other letter has been deleted from the following words. Can you use your skill and intuition to replace all of the missing letters?

Each item in the list is **part of a church**.

C_N_E_S_O_A_

B_L_ _O_E_

P_E_B_T_R_

C_O_ _S_E_

S_C_I_T_

T_A_S_P_

Sit Down Quiz

1. On the Box

What is the name of the US drama series featuring the character Sherlock Holmes where his assistant, Watson, is played by actress Lucy Liu?

2. Movie Magic

Which film featured the tagline, 'In space no one can hear you scream'?

3. Musical Mulling

Which chart-topping Canadian singer won the Eurovision Song Contest on behalf of Switzerland in 1988?

4. Around the World

What is the name of the southernmost point in Great Britain?

Loose Vowels

All of the vowels have been flushed out of the following five **printing terms**.

Can you work out what all of the words and phrases were originally?

NTL CPS

SNS SRF

PPR CS

LGNMNT

SCNDR TYPFC

Rearranging

Rearrange and join the word fragments to make five **parts of a Roman city**.

AES   AMP   CE   COU

HEA   HIT   KET   LAW

MAR   PAL   PLA   RI

RTS   TAB   TRA   TRE

ULA   UM

Trivial Thoughts

You are typically 1–2.5 cm (0.4–1 in) taller when you get out of bed than you are by the end of the day. The bones in your spine are compressed by gravity and other activities throughout the day, shortening you. Astronauts in space can grow by as much as 7.5 cm (3 in)!

☆ ☆ ☆ ☆ ☆

A baby's eyes often change colour after birth. Many babies of European ancestry are born with dark blue or slate grey eyes, which later change colour around the time of the child's first birthday. Changes can sometimes continue until the third birthday, and in rarer cases can carry on into adulthood.

☆ ☆ ☆ ☆ ☆

The Sami language of Finland, Norway and Sweden has a very large number of different words for 'reindeer'. There are around 1,000 of them, in fact!

Pottering About

The letters in each of the following **parts of a theatre** have been mixed up.

Untangle each anagram to reveal the original words.

AEFSTY ACINRTU
ADIIMORTUU
AABCEGKST
ABCLNOY
AEGLLRY
ALLSST

Solutions

Page 3
Phoebe Buffay, from 'Friends'
Mission Impossible
Yuri Gagarin
Virginia Wade

Page 4
London, Ottawa, Tokyo, Lima, Madrid, Addis Ababa

Page 5
ARCHIPELAGO
STALACTITE
STALAGMITE
GRASSLAND
PENINSULA

Page 7
GREAT WALL OF CHINA
GREAT BARRIER REEF
SYDNEY OPERA HOUSE
STATUE OF LIBERTY

Page 8
The Silence of the Lambs
Raiders of the Lost Ark
The Lord of the Rings: The Fellowship of the Ring
Saving Private Ryan
Back to the Future

Page 9
Decode by replacing A with R, B with S, C with T and so on through to replacing Y with P and Z with Q:
DICTATORSHIP
ARISTOCRACY
COMMUNALISM

MERITOCRACY
PLUTOCRACY

Page 10
ARTS AND CRAFTS
NEOCLASSICIST
PERPENDICULAR
RENAISSANCE
CORINTHIAN
BYZANTINE
CLASSICAL

Page 11
1. Ringo Starr was the oldest, and George Harrison the youngest
2. *All About Eve* (1950); *Titanic* (1997)
3. Au is gold, Ag is silver and Pt is platinum
4. Manchester United

Page 12
ICELANDIC
NORWEGIAN
UKRAINIAN
ALBANIAN
ESTONIAN
ITALIAN

Page 13
OESOPHAGUS
CAPILLARY
INTESTINE
APPENDIX
PANCREAS

Page 15
BATTLESTAR GALACTICA
WAREHOUSE THIRTEEN

THE TWILIGHT ZONE
QUANTUM LEAP

Page 16
Judgment at Nuremberg
The Great Escape
A Fistful of Dollars
The Night of the Hunter
Some Like It Hot

Page 17
Decode by replacing A with L, B with M, C with N and so on through to replacing Y with J and Z with K:
BLITZEN
PRANCER
RUDOLPH
DANCER
DASHER

Page 18
SANTORINI
ST HELENS
STROMBOLI
KRAKATOA
VESUVIUS
ETNA
FUJI

Page 19
1. 1770
2. 'Cheers', and 'Frasier', both featured Dr Frasier Crane
3. Carbon monoxide
4. Brazil have won five times, the last time in 1992

Solutions

Page 20
LEATHER
COTTON
CHINA
CORAL
PAPER
TIN

Page 21
TRINIDAD AND TOBAGO
ARGENTINA
VENEZUELA
COLOMBIA
PARAGUAY

Page 23
RECEPTACLE
THALAMUS
CARPEL
STAMEN
STIGMA
PETAL

Page 24
The Dark Knight
Cool Hand Luke
Once Upon a Time in America
Gone with the Wind
The Sixth Sense

Page 25
Decode by replacing A with W, B with X, C with Y and so on through to replacing Y with U and Z with V:
THE ARCHER
THE SCALES
THE BULL
THE CRAB

THE FISH
THE LION

Page 26
COR ANGLAIS
DIDGERIDOO
BAGPIPES
CLARINET
HORNPIPE
OBOE

Page 27
1. Josiah 'Jed' Bartlet
2. Spencer Tracy (1937 and 1938), and Tom Hanks (1993 and 1994)
3. The River Severn, at 354 km (220 miles), although some argue that it is really the River Thames
4. Blue, black, red; the bottom row is yellow and green

Page 28
CHAIN MAIL
BACKPLATE
NOSEPIECE
GAUNTLET
SURCOAT
HELMET

Page 29
ANGLERFISH
JOHN DORY
WHITEBAIT
FLOUNDER
MACKEREL

Page 31
AMSTERDAM

BARCELONA
MELBOURNE
STOCKHOLM
HELSINKI
MONTREAL

Page 32
Good Will Hunting
To Kill a Mockingbird
The Good, the Bad and the Ugly
All About Eve
The Usual Suspects

Page 33
Decode by replacing A with K, B with L, C with M and so on through to replacing Y with I and Z with J:
HUNDRED METRES
POLE VAULT
STEEPLECHASE
TRIPLE JUMP
HEPTATHLON

Page 34
MOCCASIN
PLATFORM
PLIMSOLL
STILETTO
SLIPPER
SNEAKER

Page 35
1. K2, at 8,611 m (28,251 ft)
2. *Indiana Jones and the Kingdom of the Crystal Skull*
3. Pet Shop Boys
4. Pete Sampras and Roger Federer – both have won 7

Solutions

Page 36
MICROSCOPE
DROPPER
PIPETTE
SPATULA
BEAKER
TRIPOD

Page 37
HIGH PRESSURE SODIUM
HIGH INTENSITY
MERCURY VAPOUR
ENERGY SAVING
INCANDESCENT

Page 39
BATTLESHIPS
BACKGAMMON
DRAUGHTS
MONOPOLY
SCRABBLE
REVERSI

Page 40
The Wizard of Oz
Touch of Evil
American History X
The Deer Hunter
Full Metal Jacket

Page 41
Decode by replacing A with V, B with W, C with X and so on through to replacing Y with T and Z with U:
ENGLISH BREAKFAST
LAPSANG SOUCHONG
RUSSIAN CARAVAN
ORANGE PEKOE
DARJEELING

Page 42
TAGLIATELLE
CANNELLONI
SPAGHETTI
FARFALLE
LINGUINE
RIGATONI

Page 43
1. 'Babylon 5'
2. Marty McFly
3. Brazil, Peru, Bolivia, Colombia, Ecuador, Venezuela, Guyana
4. Long Jump

Page 44
EUCALYPTUS
MAGNOLIA
APRICOT
COCONUT
SEQUOIA
ACACIA

Page 45
CHANGING OF THE GUARD
HOUSES OF PARLIAMENT
BUCKINGHAM PALACE
MILLENNIUM BRIDGE
ROYAL OBSERVATORY

Page 47
CAULIFLOWER
ASPARAGUS
SWEETCORN
CUCUMBER
MUSHROOM
CABBAGE

Page 48
The Princess Bride
Once Upon a Time in the West
The Perks of Being a Wallflower
La Dolce Vita
Into the Wild

Page 49
Decode by replacing A with X, B with Y, C with Z and so on through to replacing Y with V and Z with W:
TALLAHASSEE
SACRAMENTO
NASHVILLE
HONOLULU
BOSTON

Page 50
DAVY CROCKETT
ROBIN HOOD
AGAMEMNON
GILGAMESH
ACHILLES
BOUDICCA
LANCELOT

Page 51
1. Alyson Hannigan
2. Walt Disney
3. Romania, Ukraine, Russia, Georgia, Turkey, Bulgaria
4. Michael Phelps, for swimming

Page 52
CARAVANETTE
GOLF CART
TRACTOR
SLEDGE
TANDEM

Solutions

Page 53
BURKINA FASO
SWITZERLAND
BANGLADESH
KAZAKHSTAN
LUXEMBOURG

Page 55
FROMAGE FRAIS
RED LEICESTER
WENSLEYDALE
CAERPHILLY
GORGONZOLA
LANCASHIRE

Page 56
*Lock, Stock and Two Smoking
    Barrels*
Beauty and the Beast
V for Vendetta
The Philadelphia Story
The Lives of Others

Page 57
Decode by replacing A with F, B with
G, C with H and so on through to
replacing Y with D and Z with E:
TURQUOISE
MAGENTA
INDIGO
ORANGE
VIOLET
YELLOW

Page 58
FLAT IRON STEAK
SHOULDER TENDER
FILET MIGNON
TOP SIRLOIN

SPARE RIBS
SILVERSIDE

Page 59
1. Larry Hagman
2. *Conan the Barbarian*
3. Silver, Platinum and Mercury: Ag,
    derived from *argentum*, silver in
    Latin; Platinum, Pt, derived from
    platina, silver in Spanish; Mercury,
    Hg, derived from *hydrargyrum*,
    'liquid silver' in Greek
4. 1896 in Athens

Page 60
CHOCOLATE
LIQUORICE
ANISEED
CARAMEL
ORANGE
APPLE

Page 61
GREATER MANCHESTER
NORTHAMPTONSHIRE
BUCKINGHAMSHIRE
GLOUCESTERSHIRE
NORTH YORKSHIRE

Page 63
HOME ECONOMICS
SOCIAL SCIENCE
PHYSICS
CALCULUS
GEOMETRY
ENGLISH

Page 64
The Dark Knight Rises

One Flew Over the Cuckoo's Nest
How to Train Your Dragon
Who's Afraid of Virginia Woolf?
The Elephant Man

Page 65
Decode by replacing A with I, B with
J, C with K and so on through to
replacing Y with G and Z with H:
LLOYD GEORGE
CHAMBERLAIN
CALLAGHAN
CHURCHILL
GLADSTONE
THATCHER

Page 66
INTERNATIONAL
FINANCIAL
CONTRACT
CRIMINAL
MILITARY
PROPERTY

Page 67
1. 'Arrested Development'
2. *The American President*
3. Bryan Adams '(Everything I Do) I
    Do It for You'
4. Brazil (1958-62), Italy (1934-38)

Page 68
CELESTE
MARIMBA
TIMPANI
TOM-TOM
BONGOS
CHIMES

Solutions

Page 69
COCKER SPANIEL
JACK RUSSELL
GREAT DANE
POMERANIAN
CHIHUAHUA

Page 71
CLEMENTINE
STRAWBERRY
WATERMELON
NECTARINE
PINEAPPLE
ORANGE

Page 72
Dr Strangelove: How I Learned to Stop Worrying and Love the Bomb
The Big Lebowski
The Bridge on the River Kwai
It Happened One Night
The Bourne Ultimatum

Page 73
Decode by replacing A with I, B with J, C with K and so on through to replacing Y with G and Z with H:
MICHELANGELO
BOTTICELLI
DA VINCI
HOLBEIN
RAPHAEL

Page 74
PROTESTANTISM
CONFUCIANISM
CATHOLICISM
CALVINISM
METHODISM

MORMONISM
BUDDHISM

Page 75
1. 'Glee'
2. Alexander Pope
3. Shanghai, China, with almost 18 million inhabitants
4. France

Page 76
CHLORINE
FLUORINE
HELIUM
ARGON
RADON
NEON

Page 77
AUTOBIOGRAPHY
GRAPHIC NOVEL
ENCYCLOPEDIA
DICTIONARY
BIOGRAPHY

Page 79
BASKETBALL
WATER POLO
BOBSLEIGH
LACROSSE
ROUNDERS
CURLING
HOCKEY

Page 80
Monty Python and the Holy Grail
The Shawshank Redemption
The Man Who Shot Liberty Valance
There Will Be Blood

It's a Wonderful Life

Page 81
Decode by replacing A with Y, B with Z, C with A and so on through to replacing W with U and Z with X:
METROPOLITAN
PICCADILLY
BAKERLOO
DISTRICT
NORTHERN

Page 82
EAST CHINA
CARIBBEAN
ADRIATIC
ARABIAN
CASPIAN
AEGEAN

Page 83
1. 'Panorama', first broadcast in 1953
2. The Lord of the Rings: The Return of the King
3. Kylie Minogue
4. Great Britain, with 780. The USSR had 1,010. The ranking of the top three is the same even when you include the Winter Olympics

Page 84
ARKANSAS
COLORADO
ILLINOIS
OKLAHOMA
ALABAMA
ARIZONA

Solutions

Page 85
SOCIAL WORKER
VETERINARIAN
FIREFIGHTER
ACCOUNTANT
BEAUTICIAN

Page 87
TIPPER TRUCK
STEAMROLLER
AEROPLANE
AMBULANCE
MOTORBIKE
MINIBUS

Page 88
In the Name of the Father
The Big Sleep
Singin' in the Rain
Lagaan: Once Upon a Time in India
The Truman Show

Page 89
Decode by replacing A with F, B with G, C with H and so on through to replacing Y with D and Z with E:
ALWAYS ON MY MIND
HEARTBREAK HOTEL
LONESOME TONIGHT
SUSPICIOUS MINDS
THAT'S ALL RIGHT

Page 90
LITTLE MISS MUFFET
FAIRY GODMOTHER
PRINCE CHARMING
RUMPELSTILTSKIN
SLEEPING BEAUTY
BIG BAD WOLF

Page 91
1. Steven Moffat, who wrote 'Coupling' and later became lead writer on 'Doctor Who'
2. Three sequels: *Jaws 2*; *Jaws 3-D/ Jaws 3*; *Jaws: The Revenge*
3. Bob the Builder
4. Martina Navratilova – 6 times, from 1982 to 1987

Page 92
GUINEA PIG
ARMADILLO
ANTEATER
IGUANA
LLAMA
MOUSE

Page 93
SINGAPORE AIRLINES
AIR NEW ZEALAND
BRITISH AIRWAYS
JAPAN AIRLINES
QATAR AIRWAYS

Page 95
POISON DART FROG
BURROWING TOAD
SALAMANDER
AXOLOTL

Page 96
The Wolf of Wall Street
In the Mood for Love
Memories of Murder
Stranger on a Train
My Neighbor Totoro

Page 97
Decode by replacing A with T, B with U, C with V and so on through to replacing Y with R and Z with S:
CHARLES
WILLIAM
ALFRED
EDWARD
HENRY

Page 98
HALF HITCH
SHEEPSHANK
CROCHET
WINDSOR
DOUBLE
GRANNY

Page 99
1. Latvia
2. *Argo*
3. Proton
4. Italy, with their wins in 1938 and 1982

Page 100
WAISTCOAT
SWEATER
BLOUSE
FLEECE
KIMONO
CLOAK

Page 101
ELLIPTICAL TRAINER
RESISTANCE BAND
ROWING MACHINE
SHOULDER PRESS
CROSS TRAINER

Solutions

Page 103
EURYTHMICS
COLDPLAY
WESTLIFE
GENESIS
OASIS
QUEEN

Page 104
Requiem for a Dream
Million Dollar Baby
The Lord of the Rings: The Return of the King
Witness for the Prosecution
Dial M for Murder

Page 105
Decode by replacing A with R, B with S, C with T and so on through to replacing Y with P and Z with Q:
NAPOLEON BONAPARTE
CHARLES DE GAULLE
ALEXANDRE DUMAS
BRIGITTE BARDOT
GUSTAVE EIFFEL

Page 106
EVERGREEN
PERENNIAL
CLIMBER
SAPLING
CEREAL
FLOWER

Page 107
1. 'The Phantom of the Opera'
2. Drew Barrymore
3. Any pH less than 7.0
4. The ashes of a wooden cricket bail

Page 108
FOUNTAIN
TADPOLE
TOAD
STONES
LILY

Page 109
GENERAL MEDRANO
ALEC TREVELYAN
DOMINIC GREENE
ELLIOT CARVER
GENERAL ORLOV

Page 111
SPOT THE DIFFERENCE
WORDSEARCH
CROSSWORD
FUTOSHIKI
SUDOKU
MAZE

Page 112
Life of Brian
A Clockwork Orange
Butch Cassidy and the Sundance Kid
The Grapes of Wrath
The Maltese Falcon

Page 113
Decode by replacing A with I, B with J, C with K and so on through to replacing Y with G and Z with H:
ORPHEUS IN THE UNDERWORLD
THE BARBER OF SEVILLE
MADAME BUTTERFLY
DIDO AND AENEAS
COSI FAN TUTTE

Page 114
THE SLEEPING BEAUTY
TALES OF HOFFMAN
THE NUTCRACKER
LES SYLPHIDES
CINDERELLA
SWAN LAKE
CARMEN

Page 115
1. 1985
2. The shores of the Dead Sea, which are 418 m (1,371 ft) below sea level
3. Alessandro Volta, who gave his name to the volt
4. Roger Bannister, in 1954

Page 116
ACCELERATOR
ODOMETER
RADIATOR
SUNROOF
ENGINE
DOOR

Page 117
PARABOLIC REFLECTOR
CIRCULAR POLARIZER
POLARIZING FILTER
BATTERY CHARGER
SHUTTER RELEASE

Page 119
MAYONNAISE
AVOCADO
GHERKIN
KETCHUP
LETTUCE
MUSTARD

Solutions

Page 120
The King's Speech
Like Stars on Earth
On the Waterfront
The Secret in Their Eyes
Grave of the Fireflies

Page 121
Decode by replacing A with T, B with U, C with V and so on through to replacing Y with R and Z with S:
QUEENS PARK RANGERS
MANCHESTER UNITED
TOTTENHAM HOTSPUR
BLACKBURN ROVERS
BOLTON WANDERERS

Page 122
PLASTIC SURGERY
ANAESTHETICS
NEUROSURGERY
DERMATOLOGY
IMMUNOLOGY
PSYCHIATRY
CHIROPODY

Page 123
1. 'Band of Brothers'
2. Colin Firth
3. Methane
4. Usain Bolt

Page 124
MADAGASCAR
MAURITIUS
ETHIOPIA
ALGERIA
ERITREA
MOROCCO

Page 125
CANIS MAJOR
CANIS MINOR
CAPRICORNUS
SAGITTARIUS
CASSIOPEIA

Page 127
BARTHOLOMEW
MATTHIAS
ANDREW
THOMAS
JAMES
JUDAS

Page 128
Eternal Sunshine of the Spotless Mind
A Beautiful Mind
Black Cat, White Cat
No Country for Old Men
Fanny and Alexander

Page 129
Decode by replacing A with N, B with O, C with P and so on through to replacing Y with L and Z with M:
SEMI-SKIMMED MILK
CREME FRAICHE
FROMAGE FRAIS
WHIPPED CREAM
BUTTER

Page 130
MALT WHISKY
TRIPLE SEC
FRAMBOISE
WHITE RUM
AMARETTO

SCHNAPPS

Page 131
1. 'A Grand Day Out'
2. Hobart
3. Boolean algebra
4. Cheryl Cole

Page 132
CANADA GOOSE
WHOOPER SWAN
SHEARWATER
WILDEBEEST
CARIBOU
SALMON

Page 133
BRIEFCASE
MESSENGER
ATHLETIC
BACKPACK
RUCKSACK

Page 135
OBSERVATORY
LIGHTHOUSE
SKYSCRAPER
BOATHOUSE
CATHEDRAL
MONASTERY

Page 136
Star Wars: Episode V – The Empire Strikes Back
Mary and Max
Dog Day Afternoon
The Diving Bell and the Butterfly
Howl's Moving Castle

Solutions

Page 137
Decode by replacing A with K, B with L, C with M and so on through to replacing Y with I and Z with J:
AUSTRALIAN
JAPANESE
BRITISH
CHINESE
ITALIAN

Page 138
SWANEE WHISTLE
FRENCH HORN
HARPSICHORD
KETTLEDRUM
ACCORDION
BAGPIPES
CLARINET

Page 139
1. Lewis
2. *Beauty and the Beast*
3. Moai
4. Sunderland

Page 140
GREASEPAINT
FOUNDATION
EYELINER
LIPSTICK
MASCARA
ROUGE

Page 141
ELECTRON NEUTRINO
MUON ANTINEUTRINO
STRANGE ANTIQUARK
BOTTOM ANTIQUARK
CHARM ANTIQUARK

Page 143
DRACHMA
DOLLAR
ESCUDO
DINAR
FRANC
KRONE

Page 144
Silver Linings Playbook
Stuck In Love
He's Just Not That Into You
Forgetting Sarah Marshall
The Spectacular Now

Page 145
Decode by replacing A with I, B with J, C with K and so on through to replacing Y with G and Z with H:
HYDROGEN CHLORIDE
CARBON DIOXIDE
NITROUS OXIDE
AMMONIA
HELIUM

Page 146
CONFESSIONAL
BELL TOWER
PRESBYTERY
CLOISTER
SACRISTY
TRANSEPT

Page 147
1. 'Elementary'
2. *Alien*
3. Celine Dion
4. Lizard Point in Cornwall, England

Page 148
INITIAL CAPS
SANS SERIF
UPPER CASE
ALIGNMENT
ASCENDER
TYPEFACE

Page 149
AMPHITHEATRE
MARKETPLACE
LAW COURTS
TABULARIUM
PALAESTRA

Page 151
SAFETY CURTAIN
AUDITORIUM
BACKSTAGE
BALCONY
GALLERY
STALLS